DYNAMIC FACES

Acrylic Picture Painting for Learners

Jerry Randall

Table of Contents

CHAPTER ONE

INTRODUCTION

There are different ways to deal with fanning out a depiction. Different picture painting frameworks. Everybody has their own methodology, and all are critical. There has interminably been conversation about whether a picture ought to be made using reality or from make graphy. I won't offer you a response on that one; in the event that a magnum opus is great, the solicitation need not come up. I draw in observational concentrate however much as could be expected. According to my point of view, phenomenal capacities to draw and information on life structures are unbelievably basic.

THE BASICS OF ACRYLIC PAINT

Acrylic paint is a quick drying paint made of shade suspended in acrylic polymer emulsion. Basically, this infers it's water-dissolvable while it's wet. Right when the paint dries, regardless, it's completely water-safe. Acrylics are a shocking paint framework for amateurs. They are reasonable and open. Undoubtedly, even with the most reasonable compartments of paint out there, you can accomplish staggering outcomes. Acrylic paint supplies are in this way truly simple to remain mindful of. All you really want to need to clean your acrylic brushes is substance and water! I love utilizing acrylics since they are great for accomplishing a truly present day rich with your convincing work of art.

Acrylic paint is very much versatile. Subject to the sort of brush you use, the surface you paint on, or how much water you add, you can accomplish an extensive number of various surfaces and systems with acrylic paint. You're also ready to paint on innumerable surfaces like material, wood, paper, glass, surface, and that is just the beginning. As may be plainly obvious, acrylic paint is an incredible vehicle for youths. Chances are, you've presumably experienced painting with some sort of acrylic paint as a young. Consider this instructive movement arranging with acrylic paint. Regardless, today, we will take it to a more huge level!

ACRYLIC PAINT SUPPLY THOUGHTS

The essential supplies you'll expect for painting with acrylics are brushes, paint, and a material surface.

My primary acrylic paint supplies:

Paint:

• This strategy of acrylic paints outfits you with endless collections to work with and is a fabulous set in any case.

• I love purchasing exceptional paint in the major tones (red, yellow, and blue) and white. This engages me to blend them into any variety I pick! I love these acrylics from Winsor and Newton.

Brushes:

• Round brushes

• Decided brushes

• Range Forefront

Painting Surface:

• While I'm painting with acrylics, I like utilizing Strathmore Blended Media paper. This pack is a 400 series, and that proposes the paper is exceptionally thick. This is perfect for stacking stores of acrylic onto the page without a nonsensical proportion of paper getting.

• To give my acrylic works of art genuinely more oomph, I'll paint on material. I like this 18-pack of material sheets for two fundamental reasons:

1) There are different sizes, so you have more conspicuous flexibility with how gigantic/little you need to paint.

2) For 18 materials, this is genuinely darn honest.

In the event that these unequivocal supplies aren't available to you, no issue! As I alluded to above, acrylic paints are really flexible, and you can't turn out to be horrendous with a specific brand of plans. Tolerating for the time being that you're an acrylic painting fledgling, go ahead and use anything that plans are by and large clear for you to find.

CHAPTER TWO

SIGNIFICANT ACRYLIC PAINTING STRATEGIES

In this acrylic paint instructive movement, I will share the significant systems you genuinely need notwithstanding acrylic paints. We kept an eye on the plans you genuinely need for acrylics and next, we'll go into how to blend acrylic paint tones and learn different brush strokes to rehearsc. In the event that you truly need an entirc cach little move toward turn enlightening action of how to paint with acrylics, look at my social occasion, Current Acrylic Painting. In this class, you'll figure out a workable method for painting various subjects and will leave with a store of finished gems and heaps of acrylic painting considerations. Similarly, the most astounding point? You can watch the class with the supposition with the expectation of complimentary when you seek after a free central with Skill share.

SEEK AFTER THE CUTTING EDGE ACRYLIC PAINTING CLASS

Combination Blending

Blending acrylic paint is a fundamental expertise to rule, yet will immensely impact your acrylic craftsmanship's. One clarification that I love to blend acrylic paint as opposed to utilizing paint straight out of the chamber is that the pre-blended paint can very restrict. The vital collections you'll have the decision to paint with are the chambers that you really buy. Regardless, assuming you get to realize some basic collection blending methodologies, you can change a few level tones into any grouping you like!

The other motivation to figure out a workable method for blending acrylics is that paint out the chamber isn't unbelievably fascinating. The combinations can look level and expected, yet figuring out a workable method for blending tones will assist you with adding more conspicuous resonation to the tones you're painting with. This lifts your pieces and assists them with standing isolated from the get-together.

In this instructive action, I'll walk you through my 1 blending procedures to assist you with getting everything moving with your acrylic paints. Besides reward you essentially need four paint tones to follow. The essential tones (red, yellow, and blue) and white!

Blending Right hand Tones

Might we at some point start with the essentials. By blending the three major tones red, blue, and yellow you can make any shade of the rainbow.

Blending red and blue makes purple

Blending red and yellow makes orange

In like manner, blending yellow and blue makes green

Play with the degree of each tone and you'll see how the optional collection changes. For instance, in the event that you truly need a more lime green tone, continue to add yellow to the blue and yellow blend. This will change your green tone and make a more lime green shade. You can besides change these new optional tones that you've made by adding a smidgen of white. This will make a more pastel range like this.

BLENDING DARK

Assuming you've taken any of my Skillshare, you know that I seriously hate utilizing straight dark paint. I see that as it's simply not extremely fascinating and can look dull. My 1 method for combating this in my artworks is to make my own dark paint! To make dark, you should simply combine two integral tones as one. On the variety wheel, integral tones are the ones straightforwardly inverse of one another. My number one method for blending dark in with acrylics is to combine red and green paint as one. This is an illustration of the way red and green combine as one to make dark. The dark has a few delightful undercurrents and it is considerably more powerful than dark straight out of the cylinder. These are only two essential variety blending methods to begin with, however I urge you to mess about and let your creative mind roam free while you're blending tones. It's a truly fun method for getting to know your acrylics and an involved method for learning variety hypothesis! If you have any desire to study variety blending for acrylics go along with me for the full breakdown in my group, Current Acrylic Painting.

BRUSH CONTROL STRATEGIES WITH ACRYLIC PAINT

The subsequent stage to beginning with acrylic paint is to become familiar with your brushes. I'll walk you through some essential brush control strategies to rehearse and by and by, you'll have a smart thought of how to utilize the various sorts and sizes of brushes utilized for painting acrylics.

Sit back and relax on the off chance that your strokes are flawed this is tied in with having a great time and becoming familiar with your brushes!

Before we plunge into each unique brush type, I needed to share one of my top acrylic paint tips with you. To gain more influence with acrylic paint, add water to your brush.

This could astound you since acrylic paint is very surprising than watercolor. However, one of the advantages of acrylic paint is that it's water-dissolvable. This implies that you're ready to blend water in while the paint is wet and it won't change the design of the paint excessively.

By adding water, you'll have more command over the perfection of your strokes. On the off chance that you use acrylic paint and a dry brush, you're bound to get lopsided globs of paint in your strokes like this.

Presently how about we move into the different brush strokes and kinds of brushes for acrylic paint.

Rakish Brush Methods

The advantage of utilizing a calculated brush is that you're ready to utilize the fine mark of the brush to make more nitty gritty strokes on the page, and you can likewise utilize the thick finish to make enormous thicker strokes.

For your most memorable practice strokes, utilize the calculated edge of the brush to make thick, even lines on your page. Ensure your brush is equitably covered with color. Assuming you observe that your paint is looking smeared or lopsided, add more water.

Then, you can work on utilizing the fine mark of your calculated brush to make dainty even lines on the page.

Ultimately, you can work on utilizing both the calculated side of the brush and the fine tip by making wavy lines on your page. This procedure is just conceivable with a calculated brush, and it is an extraordinary one to rehearse!

Round Brush Strategies

Then, we'll work on utilizing a round brush. I use round brushes while I'm painting subtleties or maintain that my lines should be exact. Explore different avenues regarding the tension you are utilizing with the round brush. Utilize a lighter tension for meager lines and a heavier strain for thicker lines.

Thick Brush Methods

The last brush I suggest rehearsing with is a huge brush with thick fibers. These sorts of brushes are perfect for accomplishing surface that you can get with acrylic paint. I love when you're ready to see the finished fibers come through on the page. Different brush procedures will give you various surfaces. The following are a couple of you can attempt:

Work on spotting your brush on the page to get surfaces like this. To get a painterly brushstroke look, work on utilizing a dry brush and painting even dry strokes on the page. There is such a lot of space for adaptability and imagination with regards to acrylic paint. This is only a leaping off highlight provide you with the essentials of acrylics. I trust this instructional exercise has enabled you to pick your acrylic paints up and get everything rolling! To plunge profound into the universe of acrylic paint or on the other hand to figure out how to paint explicit themes.

CHAPTER THREE

MAKE GRAPHY

Laying out a representation from make graphy enjoys benefits and weaknesses. One of the significant entanglements is the risk of giving to much consideration to the subtleties. Similarity doesn't rely upon the subtleties yet on enormous volumes. Recall that old fashioned make graph. You realize entirely well who will be who, albeit the countenances are no greater than a fourth of an inch. Keep it basic and be intense with what you say. A benefit of working with make graphs is that you simply pick the shot you like most out of a series. Before you start, it is essential to give extraordinary consideration to the make graphy meeting, and furthermore to the printing. The two huge make graphs are a similar size as the picture on the material. The left is marginally unfocused to keep away from interruption from subtleties. On the easel is the extended material. I utilize red colored pencil. The dark graphite of an ordinary pencil will constantly appears through all layers of oil paint. Here I fixed the drawing with an exceptionally slim layer of shellac. In some cases I apply a slight covering of an alkyd medium. On top, in acrylic I paint an under painting in crude sienna. On the off chance that I get lost I generally can eliminate a layer of oil to see the fundamental drawing and under painting.

Painting

The real work of art of the picture is going to start. I start the day right on time by setting up my range, which is finished with extraordinary consideration. I blend the skin tones and consistently utilize a test strip to really look at the combination. Before I begin painting, I rub the material with an unbiased oil medium. Then, at that point, the material is semi-immersed and the material "gets" the paint from my brush all the more without any problem a little bit of white. This will create a more pastel palette like this.

Mixing Black

If you've taken any of my Skill share classes, you know that I'm not a fan of using straight black paint. I find that it's just not very interesting and can look dull. My favorite way to combat this in my paintings is to create my own black paint! To create black, all you have to do is mix two complementary colors together. On the color wheel, complementary colors are the ones directly opposite of each other.

My favorite way to mix black with acrylics is to mix red and green paint together. Here's an example of how red and green mix together to make black. The black has some beautiful undertones and it is much more dynamic than black straight out of the tube. These are just two basic color mixing techniques to get started with, but I encourage you to play around and let your imagination run wild when you're mixing colors. It's a really fun way to get to know your acrylics and a hands-on way to learn color theory! If you want to learn more about color mixing for acrylics join me for the full breakdown in my class, Modern Acrylic Painting.

BRUSH CONTROL TECHNIQUES WITH ACRYLIC PAINT

The next step to getting started with acrylic paint is to get comfortable with your brushes. I'll walk you through some basic brush control techniques to practice and by the end you'll have a good idea of how to use the different types and sizes of brushes used for painting acrylics.

Don't worry if your strokes aren't perfect, this is all about having fun and getting comfortable with your brushes! Before we dive into each different brush type, To get more control with acrylic paint, add water to your brush. This might surprise you since acrylic paint is totally different than watercolor. But one of the benefits of acrylic paint is that it's water-soluble. This means that you're able to mix water in while the paint is wet and it won't change the structure of the paint too much. By adding water, you'll have more control over the smoothness of your strokes. If you use acrylic paint and a dry brush, you're more likely to get uneven globs of paint in your strokes like this.

Now let's move into the different brush strokes and types of brushes for acrylic paint.

ANGULAR BRUSH TECHNIQUES

The benefit of using an angled brush is that you're able to use the fine point of the brush to make more detailed strokes on the page, and you can also use the thick end to make large thicker strokes.

For your first practice strokes, use the angled edge of the brush to create thick, even lines on your page. Make sure your brush is evenly coated with pigment. If you find that your paint is looking blotchy or uneven, add more water.

Next, you can practice using the fine point of your angled brush to create thin even lines on the page. Lastly, you can practice using both the angled side of the brush and the fine tip by creating wavy lines on your page. This technique is only possible with an angled brush, and it is a great one to practice!

ROUND BRUSH TECHNIQUES

Next, we'll practice using a round brush. I use round brushes when I'm painting details or want my lines to be precise. Experiment with the pressure you are using with the round brush. Use a lighter pressure for thin lines and a heavier pressure for thicker lines.

CHAPTER FOUR

THICK BRUSH TECHNIQUES

The last brush I recommend practicing with is a large brush with thick bristles. These types of brushes are great for achieving texture that you can only get with acrylic paint. I love when you're able to see the textured bristles come through on the page. Different brush techniques will give you diffcrent textures. Here are a few you can try:

Practice dabbing your brush on the page to get textures like this.

To get a painterly brushstroke look, practice using a dry brush and painting even dry strokes on the page.

There is so much room for flexibility and creativity when it comes to acrylic paint. This is just a jumping-off point to give you the basics of acrylics. If you want to dive deep into the world of acrylic paint or if you want to learn how to paint specific motifs, I'd love for you to join me in my class, Modern Acrylic Painting. In this class, we explore ten separate acrylic styles and you'll finish the class with a stack of brand new paintings. This class is for all levels. Whether you're an acrylic painting beginner or an experienced artist, you'll discover the joy of acrylic painting and learn how to infuse modern techniques into this easy-to-use medium. Painting a portrait from make graphy has advantages and disadvantages. One of the major pitfalls is the danger of paying too much attention to the details. Likeness does not depend on the details but on large volumes. Remember that old school make . You know perfectly well who is who, although the faces are no bigger than a quarter of an inch. Often too much detail has a devastating effect on a portrait. Keep it simple and be bold with what you say. An advantage of working with make s is that you just choose the shot you like most out of a series. Before you start, it is important to pay great attention to the make graphy session, and also to the printing.

The first image shows several copies of the face around my canvas on my easel. The two large make s are the same size as the portrait on the canvas. The left is slightly unfocused to avoid distraction from details.

Preparation

On the easel is the stretched canvas. I've transferred the image by using a grid distribution on the make as well as on the canvas. I use red crayon. The black graphite of a normal pencil will always shows through all layers of oil paint. Here I fixed the drawing with a very thin layer of shellac. Sometimes I apply a thin coating of an alkyd medium. On top, in acrylic I paint an under painting in raw sienna. If I get lost I always can remove a layer of oil to see the basic drawing and under painting.

Painting

The actual painting of the portrait is about to begin. I start the day early by setting up my palette, which is done with great care. I mix the skin colors and always use a test strip to check the mixture. Before I start painting, I rub the canvas with a neutral oil medium. Then the linen is semi- saturated and the canvas "receives" the paint from my brush more easily.

THE END

www.ingramcontent.com/pod-product-compliance
Lightning Source LLC
Chambersburg PA
CBHW072225290526
45794CB00007B/2888